NOVELLO HANDEL EDITION
General Editor Watkins Shaw

Let God arise

Anthem for soprano & tenor soli,
SATB & orchestra

Edited by Janet Beat

vocal score

Order No: NOV 072320

NOVELLO PUBLISHING LIMITED
14 –15 Berners Street, London W1T 3LJ UK

PREFACE

Let God arise is one of the twelve anthems which Handel wrote for the Duke of Chandos in the period 1716-1718. At the Duke's seat, Cannons (near Edgware, Middlesex), a small musical establishment was maintained, enabling Divine Service to be rendered with vocal and instrumental music. Some of Handel's anthems appear to have been written before the Duke's chapel was completed, and these may have first been heard in the nearby parish church of St Lawrence.

After his Cannons period Handel recast this particular anthem for the Chapel Royal, making it a shorter work in A major for five-part chorus; but this is strictly speaking not a Chandos anthem, though sometimes reckoned as such.

Sources

A London, British Library (Reference Division), RM 20.d.6, ff. 43-76 (the composer's autograph).

B Loc. cit., RM 19.g.1, Vol. 2, ff. 63-95 (in the hand of Smith 11 in Larsen's classification).

C Loc. cit., RM 19.g.1, Vol. 3, ff. 58-83v (in the hand of J. C. Smith the elder).

D Tenbury Wells, Worcs., St Michael's College MS 882, ff. 2-50 (in the hand of J. C. Smith the elder; formerly belonging to Thomas Chilcot, organist of Bath).

E London, Royal College of Music, MS 244 (in a hand similar to that of Smith 5).

F London, British Library (Reference Division), Add. MS 29418.

G New Brunswick, Rutgers University Library, MS 2145, Vol. 9, pp. 2-9 (in the hand of Jos: Ffish, Darwen, near Blackburn, Lancs., 1772. See Martin Picker, 'Handeliana in the Rutgers University Library', *Journal of the Rutgers University Library*, December 1965, pp. 5-12).

H Chicago University, Joseph Regenstein Library, MS 437 (a set of vocal and instrumental parts. See Hans Lenneberg and Lawrence Libin, 'Unknown Handel Sources in Chicago', *Journal of the American Musicological Society*, Vol. 22 (1969), pp. 85-100).

The anthem was published as part 74 of *The Works of G. F. Handel*, edited in score by Samuel Arnold, London, 1787-1797.

References do not always distinguish between the present (B flat major) version and the later Chapel Royal (A major) version, and therefore it may be useful to state that the following refer to the latter:

British Library (Reference Division), RM 20.g.4, Add. MS 29998, Egerton MS 2911; Cambridge, Fitzwilliam Museum, Barrett Lennard Collection, MS 812; Manchester Public Library, Flower Collection, MS 130 Hd4 v. 47; Bentley, Hants, the Collection of Gerald Coke, Esq.; Chicago University, Joseph Regenstein Library, MS 437. The A major version constituted part 75 of Samuel Arnold's edition, and it was included in *The complete score of ten anthems chiefly for the Chapel of . . . the late James Duke of Chandos . . .*, Vol. 3, Wright and Wilkinson, London, *c*. 1783.

Text

Both Samuel Arnold and **H** above include, besides the version given here, alternative settings of 'Like as the smoke' (No. 3) and 'O sing unto God' (No. 5), derived from the Chapel Royal version. These cannot be thought of as serious alternatives in the context of the B flat major version and are omitted here.

Otherwise the major disagreements among the sources relate to the Symphony. In the first place, **B, C, D,** and **F,** together with Arnold, contain only the second (*allegro*) movement. This is no doubt because the *a tempo ordinario* movement was an afterthought of Handel's, marked in his writing in **A** 'To be played before the symphony of Let God arise'. In the second place, Handel has marked the oboe part of the *allegro* movement 'ad libitum', and both **D** and Arnold have acted on this by omitting the oboe part—which does indeed add nothing of thematic significance and merely fills out the harmonies of a trio-sonata texture. In the third place, **C** treats the instrumental bass of the *allegro* differently from other secondary sources, including **D,** the work of the same scribe. This is discussed in a separate note below.

Otherwise discrepancies between **A** and the other sources are minimal (accidentals missed or supplied, occasional slips, basso continuo figures missed or supplied) and have not been collated. The copy-text of the present edition is that of **A,** any comments on which are given as footnotes in the body of the text.

Handel took his literary text from Psalm 68, vv. 1-4, Psalm 76, v. 6, and Psalm 68, v. 19, in the Book of Common Prayer, the orthography and punctuation of which has been followed here.

Editorial procedure

In the following matters, this edition conforms to the practice of the series of which it is a part:

1   Time-signatures. $\frac{4}{4}$ in this edition replaces Handel's C.

iii

2   Accidentals and ties. Accidentals not found in **A**, whether or not they are supplied in any secondary source, are placed in square brackets. Cancelling accidentals within the bar have been supplied, in accordance with modern practice, where Handel did not use them, and a few have also been supplied in immediately succeeding bars for the benefit of today's performers. Editorial ties are shown thus: ⌒ . It has not been thought necessary to distinguish as editorial those ties omitted by Handel in the voice parts where a syllable is sustained, e.g. No. 8, bass voice, bars 23-24, or No. 5, alto and tenor voices, bar 48, within which Handel wrote minims, thus: 𝅗𝅥· 𝅗𝅥· ♩♪

                        prai   -   [ses]

3   Marks of speed, style, dynamics and instrumentation. Those in the autograph are reproduced, supplemented by editorial suggestions in square brackets. Handel's usage in naming instruments ('haut' for oboe, 'basson' for bassoon, etc.) has been modernized.

4   Clef signs. Handel used the appropriate C clefs for his soprano, alto and tenor voices.

5   The division into numbered movements is editorial.

6   Verbal underlay. It was not Handel's practice to write out in full all the words with their many repetitions. His intentions in this work are not in doubt, and the words are printed complete without editorial differentiation.

[Handel did not generally use slurs to show verbal underlay — but neither did he join his quavers, etc., except when sung to a single syllable. Slurs in this edition are simply used to help make the underlay clear, but they have not been applied to long phrases. *General Editor.*]

The keyboard part

The textures of the orchestral score are such that it is impossible either to show them clearly in short score or to represent them with much fidelity in a keyboard transcription. Under these circumstances the keyboard part given in this vocal score is no more than a free arrangement of the orchestral parts, and is intended merely as support for rehearsal purposes. Any occasional editorial filling-in is distinguished by small-size notes. In No. 4 it has proved possible to give some indication of the instrumentation. But whatever freedom has been observed, one feature has been faithfully reflected in accordance with the principles of this series, namely, that the lower stave of the keyboard part provides the strict text of the (organ) basso continuo, it being understood that in No. 3, bars 3-4 and 13-14, and No. 5, bars 40-43, the notes with upward stems do not relate to this. The G clef has been used for *bassetti* passages in the basso continuo expressed by Handel in G or C clefs, with the exception of bars 20-23 of No. 7, where too many leger lines would be needed.

Use of solo voices

Handel nowhere marked his voice parts as either solo or chorus. Nos. 3 and 4 are obviously for solo voices, and are so treated in the secondary sources. His choral forces at Cannons were modest, one surviving list naming three trebles, one alto, two counter-tenors, one tenor, and one bass. These would be able to deal with flexible passage-work in a way which a larger choir cannot. If, then, a choir of any size is used today one may go further and treat No. 6 as a solo quartet (as Arnold does), and use a pair of solo voices for No. 5 as far as letter B and a reduced choir to the end of the movement. Conductors should treat these suggestions on their merits in relation to the scale of performance.

Note on the instrumental bass of the Symphony, bar 27 to the end

In **A** Handel allots two staves to his instrumental bass, the upper for cello and bassoon, the lower for double bass and organ. These are identical as far as bar 39 where, on the lower stave, he wrote a crotchet *B♭* and nothing else, not even rests. He continued to leave this lower stave blank until bar 59 where, finding himself on a new page, he wrote his instrumental bass on the lower stave, leaving the upper one blank for the time being. However, at bar 62 (in the middle of a page), he seems to have recollected himself, and wrote the note-head (no stem) *d* on the first beat and then left a blank, while starting at the same point to enter the semiquaver figure on the upper stave. From this point to the end nothing more is entered on the lower stave. The result may be expressed thus:

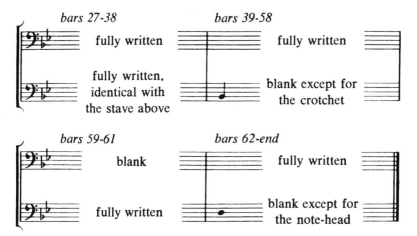

In **C** J. C. Smith treats what is seen at bar 39 as a hint to extract a double bass/ organ part which is not identical with the cello/bassoon part. Following the crotchet *B♭* in bar 39 he fills up the lower stave with rests until, on his own discretion, he reintroduces the double bass/organ at bar 45, which he then continues unbroken

to the end. But if there is anything in this, it would seem that the double bass/organ should have been dropped again after the first note of bar 62. Thereafter, however, puzzles arise; and it is no doubt because of these that Smith kept the double bass/organ part going continuously from bar 45. Yet if the double bass/organ plays in bars 62-65 and in 74-78, there is no reason to omit it in bars 39-44. All secondary sources other than **C** coalesce the two staves in question and use the expression 'tutti bassi', making no distinction of treatment.

The casual form in which Handel left **A** in this respect is probably without significance. But in a texture which is so patently that of a trio-sonata (from which indeed this movement may well have been borrowed) a double bass seems out of place, and despite Handel's labelling of his staves the omission of the double bass—not, of course, the organ—from bar 27 to the end of the Symphony may be suggested.

Acknowledgements

I am grateful to the authorities of the British Library for permission to base this edition on Handel's autograph score, and to them and all other library authorities for permitting access to the secondary manuscript sources listed above. I am grateful to Watkins Shaw for advice in various ways and also for his suggestion that the opening instrumental movement should be given in open score and arranging this with the publishers.

JANET BEAT
1978

DURATION ABOUT 23 MINUTES

Full score and instrumental material
are available on hire.

LET GOD ARISE

Anthem for the Duke of Chandos

Edited by Janet Beat

G. F. HANDEL

1 Symphony

*Handel also wrote, in pencil, 'Larghetto' but without cancelling his original direction.

20205

2

*Handel appears to place 'Adagio' above the third beat.

† For a discussion of this bass line, see note on p. v

4

39

42

45

48

51

B

54

[senza fag.]

57

60

[con fag.]

6

63

66

69

72

75

[tutti continuando]

78

C   Adagio

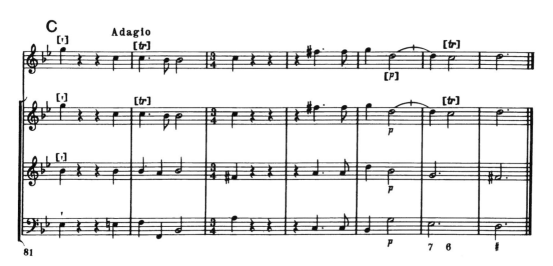

81

8

2 Let God arise
Chorus

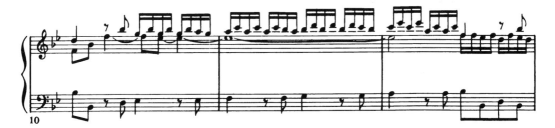

11

10

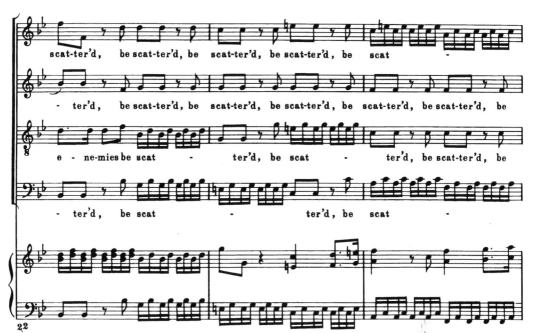

1) Bar 26, all voices. Handel unthinkingly wrote ♩♩♩♩ to 'scatter'd his'.

12

34

36

14

44

49

16

al - so that hate him, flee, _____ flee, let them

al - so that hate him, flee, flee, _____ let them

al - so that hate him, flee, flee, flee, let them

al - so that hate him, flee, _____ let them

74

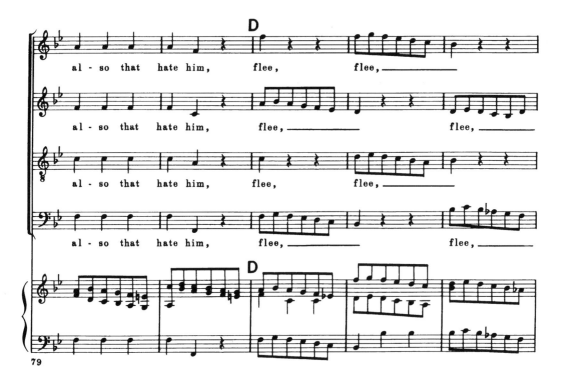

D

al - so that hate him, flee, flee, _____

al - so that hate him, flee, _____ flee, _____

al - so that hate him, flee, flee, _____

al - so that hate him, flee, _____ flee, _____

D

79

18

flee, flee, flee be - fore him.

flee, flee, flee be - fore him.

flee, flee, flee be - fore— him.

flee, flee, flee be - fore him.

3 Like as the smoke
Solo

1) Bar 4, oboe. **A** has b^1.

drive them a - way, so shalt thou drive them a - way, so shalt thou

drive _____

them, so shalt thou drive them a - way,

like as the smoke va - nish-eth,

so shalt thou drive _____

40

them, so shalt thou drive them a-way,

43

so shalt thou drive ____ them a - way,

47

so shalt thou drive ___ them a - way; like as

50

2) Bar 45, Solo voice. Rhythm thus in **A** ; but cf. bars 30, 48 and 51.

wax   melt - eth at the   fire, ___   melt - eth at the

fire, ___   so let   the un-god - ly   per - ish,

per - ish   at the pre - sence of   God,   at the   pre - sence   of

God,   so let   the un-god-ly   per - ish,

cello

organ and c.b.

per - ish, per - ish, per - ish, per - ish, so

69

let the un-god - ly __ per - ish at the pre - sence of

73

God.

77

[tr]

81

4 Let the righteous be glad
Solo

1) Bar 21, Solo voice. Handel either did not notice, or did not care about, the inconsistency between his phrasing here, and in bar 30.

and re-joice be-fore

God,   let the right-eous be glad,

let the   right-eous be_ glad, _____

and re - joice, _____

28

and re-joice be - fore

God ; let them al - so be mer-ry and

joy - ful, let them al - so be mer - ry and joy - ful, mer - ry and joy - ful,

let them al - so be mer - ry and joy - ful, joy - -

joy - - - - - ful, joy -

- - ful, mer - ry and joy - ful, let them al-so be mer-ry and

joy - ful, mer-ry and joy - - ful.

5 O sing unto God
Duet and Chorus[1]

1) See discussion on use of solo voices, p.v

2) See discussion on use of solo voices, p.v

36

38

6 Praised be the Lord
Quartet[1]

SOPRANO

ALTO — Prais - ed be the

TENOR — Prais - ed be the

BASS

Prais - ed be the

Lord,

Lord,

Prais - ed be the

1) See discussion on use of solo voices, p.v

7 At thy rebuke, O God
Chorus

44

48

50

MICHAEL HURD

Jonah-man Jazz

A CANTATA-MUSICAL
FOR UNISON VOICES
AND PIANO
WITH GUITAR CHORDS

JAZZ TESTAMENT

Now it is possible to combine Michael Hurd's Bible-based 'pop' cantatas in a modern equivalent of a cycle of Medieval Mystery Plays. The composer has devised Instructions for an 'elastic' musical and provided a new setting of William Cowper's famous Olney hymn, *God moves in a mysterious way* to introduce and link the cantatas under the title **Jazz Testament**. The instructions and hymn are available as a leaflet from Novello & Co. Ltd. (Cat. No. 16 0205).

NOVELLO

Order No: NOV 200002

COMPOSER'S NOTE

I hope that performers will adopt the free-and-easy style usually associated with 'pop' in its various forms, and not stand too much in awe of the notes as printed. There would seem to be no reason why any suitable group of jazz instrumentalists should not use the piano score as a basis for improvisation. Above all: there is no point in approaching the work in any other spirit than the determination to have fun. If so moved, let hands clap, fingers click, and voices add yelps of encouragement.

The following parts are
available for hire only:

Flute / Piccolo

Oboe

Bass Clarinet in B♭

Alto Saxophone in E♭

Trumpet in B♭

Trombone

Double Bass

The first performance of this work was given by Eric J. Jones and the boys of the Bexley-Erith Technical High School, in December 1966.

Duration 10 minutes

Reprint March 1967, with slight revisions

For Margaret

JONAH-MAN JAZZ

Words and Music by
MICHAEL HURD

1

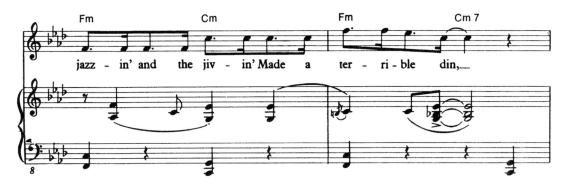

Lord when he heard it said: 'Bless_ my soul!'_

The peo - ple would - n't lis - ten, Danced

night an' day; No time_ for work, No time to pray. They

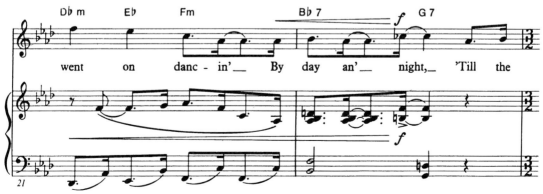

went on danc - in'_ By day an'_ night,_ 'Till the

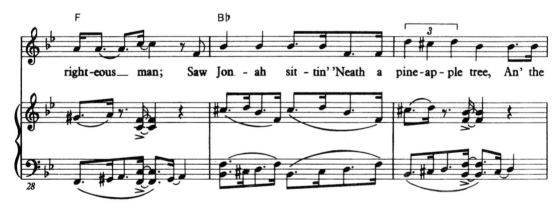

Jonah-man Jazz

4

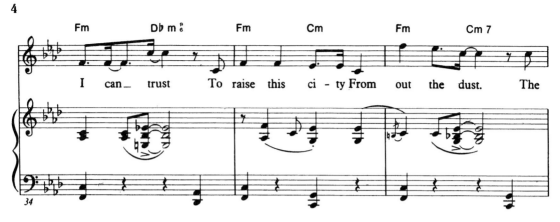

I can＿ trust To raise this ci - ty From out the dust. The

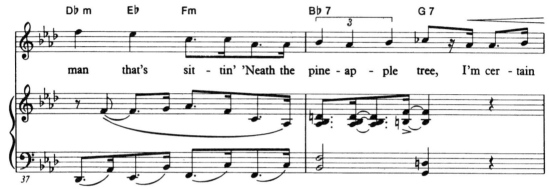

man that's sit - tin' 'Neath the pine - ap - ple tree, I'm cer - tain

sure, Sure, sure, Is the man＿ for me.'

Jonah-man Jazz

Narrator *(spoken):* And the Lord spake unto Jonah with a loud voice, saying:

2

'Jon - ah, Jon - ah,
Lis - ten to me, Jon — ah; Lis - ten while I tell you Of a
plan I have in mind. A ci - ty danc - in', Danc-in' and ro - manc - in',
All too ob-vious-ly To vir - tue must be blind. Take my warn - in'

Jonah-man Jazz

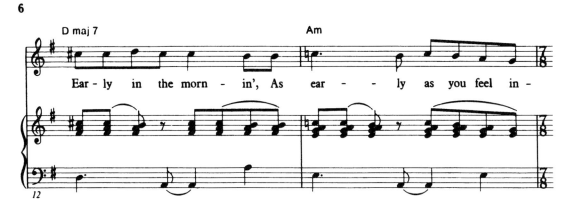

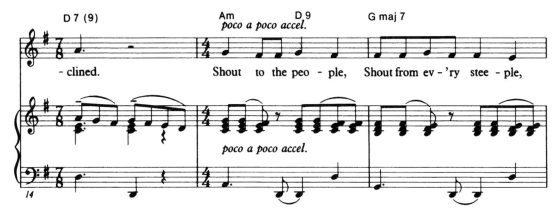

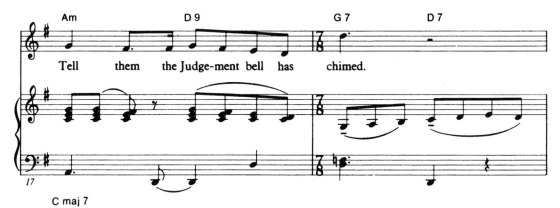

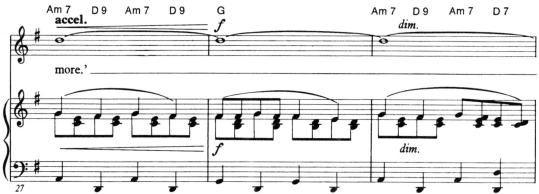

Jonah-man Jazz

8

8

Narrator: But Jonah feared to do as the Lord commanded. He turned instead and ran. He ran until he came to the sea. There he found a boat, and a man standing by. And to that man he said:

Jonah-man Jazz

9

Jonah-man Jazz

10

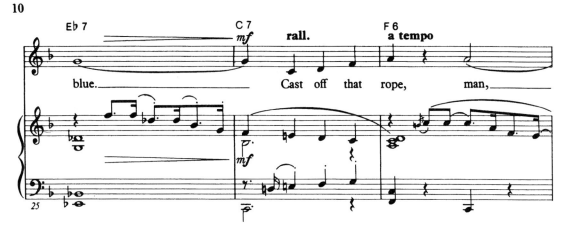

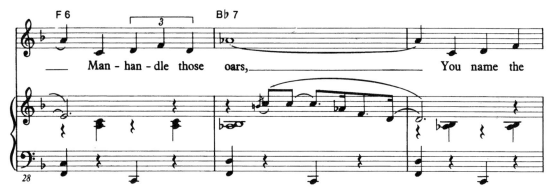

Jonah-man Jazz

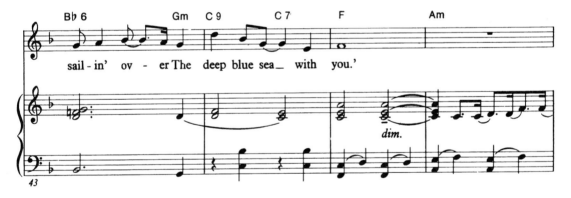

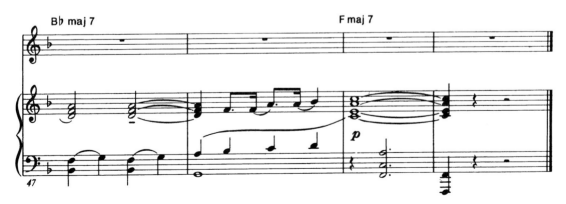

Jonah-man Jazz

Narrator: And so the boat set sail, and Jonah thought he would escape the eye of the Lord. But as they sailed, and night drew on, a strange thing came to pass.

4

waves grew high,— The ship be-gan to roll, The wind blew strong And the

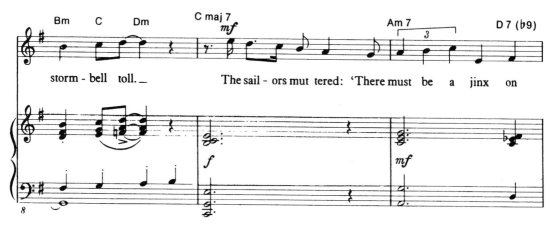

storm - bell toll. _ The sail - ors mut tered: 'There must be a jinx on

And the barking of the farmer's dog,
And felt the damp of the river fog,
That rises after the sun goes down.

It was twelve by the village clock,
When he crossed the bridge into Medford town.
He heard the crowing of the cock,

And under the alders that skirt its edge,
Now soft on the sand, now loud on the ledge,
Is heard the tramp of his steed as he rides.

He has left the village and mounted the steep,
And beneath him, tranquil and broad and deep,
Is the Mystic, meeting the ocean tides;

That was all! And yet, through the gloom and the light,
The fate of a nation was riding that night;
And the spark struck out by that steed, in his flight,
Kindled the land into flame with its heat.

A hurry of hoofs in a village street,
A shape in the moonlight, a bulk in the dark,
And beneath, from the pebbles, in passing, a spark
Struck out by a steed flying fearless and fleet:

He springs to the saddle, the bridle he turns,
But lingers and gazes, till full on his sight
A second lamp in the belfry burns!

And lo! as he looks, on the belfry's height
A glimmer, and then a gleam of light!

And turned and tightened his saddle-girth; As it rose above the graves on the hill,
But mostly he watched with eager search Lonely and spectral and sombre
The belfry-tower of the Old North Church, and still.

Meanwhile, impatient to mount and ride,
Booted and spurred, with a heavy stride
On the opposite shore walked Paul Revere.

Now he patted his horse's side,
Now gazed at the landscape far and near,
Then, impetuous, stamped the earth,

Of the place and the hour,
 and the secret dread
Of the lonely belfry and the dead;
For suddenly all his thoughts are bent

On a shadowy something far away,
Where the river widens to meet the bay,—
A line of black that bends and floats
On the rising tide, like a bridge of boats.

Beneath, in the churchyard, lay the dead,
In their night-encampment on the hill,
Wrapped in silence so deep and still
That he could hear, like a sentinel's tread,

The watchful night-wind, as it went
Creeping along from tent to tent,
And seeming to whisper, "All is well!"
A moment only he feels the spell

Masses and moving shapes of shade,—
By the trembling ladder, steep and tall,
To the highest window in the wall,

Where he paused to listen and look down
A moment on the roofs of the town,
And the moonlight flowing over all.

Then he climbed the tower
  of the Old North Church,
By the wooden stairs, with stealthy tread,

To the belfry-chamber overhead,
And startled the pigeons from their perch
On the sombre rafters, that round him made

The sound of arms, and the tramp of feet,
And the measured tread of the grenadiers,
Marching down to their boats on the shore.

Meanwhile, his friend, through alley and street,
Wanders and watches with eager ears,
Till in the silence around him he hears

A phantom ship, with each mast and spar
Across the moon like a prison bar,
And a huge black hulk, that was magnified

He said to his friend, "If the British march
By land or sea from the town to-night,
Hang a lantern aloft in the belfry arch
Of the North Church tower
    as a signal light,—

One, if by land, and two, if by sea;
And I on the opposite shore will be,
Ready to ride and spread the alarm
Through every Middlesex village and farm,
For the country folk to be up and to arm."

Listen, my children, and you shall hear
Of the midnight ride of Paul Revere,
On the eighteenth of April, in Seventy-five;
Hardly a man is now alive
Who remembers that famous day and year.

To Eugene Pettinelli, my friend, who has been there
for me from the beginning
—C.S.

For his assistance, I'd like to thank Mr. Herb Jacobs—C.S.

Paul Revere's Ride: The Landlord's Tale
Illustrations copyright ©2003 by Charles Santore
This is an officially licensed edition first published in 2014 by Cider Mill Press Book Publishers LLC

13-Digit ISBN: 978-1-60433-493-7
10-Digit ISBN: 1-60433-493-2

This book may be ordered by mail from the publisher. Please include $5.99 for postage and handling.
Please support your local bookseller first!

Books published by Cider Mill Press Book Publishers are available at special discounts for bulk purchases in the United States by corporations, institutions, and other organizations. For more information, please contact the publisher.

Applesauce Press is an imprint of
Cider Mill Press Book Publishers
"Where Good Books Are Ready for Press"
PO Box 454
12 Spring Street
Kennebunkport, Maine 04046

Visit us online!
cidermillpress.com

Typography: ITC Caslon 224 & Old Claude LP
Printed in China

3 4 5 6 7 8 9 0

Paul Revere's Ride

THE LANDLORD'S TALE

by Henry Wadsworth Longfellow
Illustrated by Charles Santore

APPLESAUCE PRESS

KENNEBUNKPORT, MAINE